THE END
of OUR FAITH

THE END
OF OUR FAITH

DEVELOPING THE CONFIDENCE THAT
GETS PRAYERS ANSWERED

by

Lynne Hammond

Harrison House
Tulsa, Oklahoma

05 04 03 02 01   10 9 8 7 6 5 4 3 2 1

The End of Our Faith—
Developing the Confidence That Gets Prayers Answered
ISBN 1-57794-392-9
Copyright © 2001 by Lynne Hammond
Mac Hammond Ministries
P.O. Box 29469
Minneapolis, Minnesota 55429

Published by Harrison House, Inc.
P. O. Box 35035
Tulsa, Oklahoma 74153

DEDICATION

To all the staff at Living Word Christian
Center who have prayed, confessed
and believed with me and Mac
for God's highest and best.

CONTENTS

INTRODUCTION

Did you know it's easy to stop somewhere in the middle of the plan of God and never see the final outcome you desire?

God's plan won't just drop in your lap like an apple falling off a tree. You grow into it day by day as you continually feed on God's Word and fellowship with Him.

Eventually that Word will begin to govern how you think and how you speak. You'll become so grounded in it that nothing will be able to shake you or move you off your stance of faith. When that happens, you can be sure God's plan will be fulfilled in you.

I want to help you get to that place in God. I want you to be able to come before God's throne on a daily basis and lay hold of His plan—not only for yourself, but for the great harvest of souls God so desires in this time and hour.

That's what I'm believing for you as you take the time to read this book!

—*Lynne Hammond*

Confess your faults one to another,
and pray one for another, that ye may
be healed. The effectual fervent prayer
of a righteous man availeth much.

JAMES 5:16

1

GET FERVENT ABOUT
YOUR ANSWER!

1

GET FERVENT ABOUT
YOUR ANSWER!

If you're like most people, you can think of many times in your life when you prayed for something and never saw the answer. You never saw the results you were believing for—or what I call "the end of your faith"—come to pass. That's a problem God never intended for you to have. He has provided a way for you to get answers every single time you pray according to the Word! He wants all your prayers to be effective.

GOD WANTS ALL YOUR PRAYERS TO BE EFFECTIVE.

The Fervent Prayer of a Righteous Man

What are the elements of effective prayer?

James 5:16 tells us. It says: **The effectual fervent prayer of a righteous man availeth much.** The *Amplified* version says it this way: **The earnest (heartfelt, continued) prayer of a righteous man makes tremendous power available [dynamic in its working].**

We see here two characteristics that effective "pray-ers" possess: they are righteous, and they are fervent.

That first characteristic might scare some people. They might say, "Oh dear, I'm not good enough to qualify as a righteous person." If you have that thought, let me remind you that it's not your goodness that makes you righteous—it's Jesus' goodness. We

> IT'S NOT YOUR GOODNESS THAT MAKES YOU RIGHTEOUS—IT'S JESUS' GOODNESS.

don't pray in our name; we pray in His name. By simply believing in Him, we qualify as righteous because our faith puts us in Him.

Every time you pray, remind yourself of that. Say to yourself, "He who knew no sin was made to be sin for me so that I could be made the righteousness of God in Christ. (2 Cor. 5:21.) So my prayer is the prayer of the righteous!"

The second characteristic of answered prayer that we see in James 5:16 is fervency. The righteous person in this verse isn't just saying something with his mouth. He has a fire within him. You see, fervor isn't something you project with your *voice;* it's something that comes forth from your *heart.* The truth is, you can sound bold with your voice and yet be quivering with fear on the inside. Thus, fervency is a condition of the heart, and it comes through a constant tuning of the heart to heaven.

FERVOR COMES FORTH FROM YOUR *HEART*.

Pray God's Plan, Not Your Problem

How do you tune your heart to heaven? By going to God's Word and finding out what He has to say about your situation. You stop praying about the problem all the time, and you start praying about God's plan for you.

However, if you're going to pray fervently about that plan, you'll have to do more than just *know* it. You'll have to meditate on it until God's plan is bigger on the inside of you than the problem is.

STOP PRAYING ABOUT THE PROBLEM AND START PRAYING ABOUT GOD'S PLAN FOR YOU.

You're probably very familiar with what happens when you meditate on the problem all the time. You can get so fervent about your problem that you just have to do something— and that "something" is usually to *cry!*

But you can change that by meditating on God's promises. If you're not sure what promises to study, just read your Bible until some Scripture hits your heart in a special way and blesses you so much that you just can't get away from it. When that happens, you'll find that every time you go to the Word and try to study other Scriptures, you'll have a hard time doing it. You'll think, *Now it's time for me to read something else in the Bible.* But each time you do, your heart will be drawn back to this particular Scripture that just keeps on blessing you.

Why is it so difficult to go on to other Scriptures in the Word at times like this? Because the Holy Ghost is moving on that particular Scripture. He is quickening that verse to you. And if you'll keep feeding on it, it will "rev up" your spirit every time you read it. After a while, you'll reach the place of fervency, the place from which you need to pray. God's plan for your situation will grow inside of you until it's so big in your spirit that you think you're going to burst.

You'll get so fervent in your heart concerning the answer to your prayers that you won't be able to sit in your seat—you'll just have to do something. That's the time to open your mouth and begin to praise God for your answer because it is sure to come!

For he performeth the thing
that is appointed for me: and many
such things are with him.

JOB 23:14

2

GOD WILL PERFORM HIS
APPOINTED PLAN FOR YOU

2

GOD WILL PERFORM HIS APPOINTED PLAN FOR YOU

"Sister Lynne," you may say, "when it comes to finding scriptural promises, I don't even know where to begin." That's all right-I'll help you by sharing one particular Scripture that is always a faith builder for me. This Scripture is strong on my heart when I am praying for a situation. It's Job 23:14, and it's one of those Scriptures that has made *me* fervent.

**For he performeth the thing that is appointed
for me: and many such things are with him.**

JOB 23:14 IS
ONE OF THOSE
SCRIPTURES
THAT HAS MADE
ME FERVENT.

I'm telling you, this is a
verse you can "plant your
flag" on and claim for the
answer to your prayer!

I love this Scripture
because it's talking about
Job when he was in the
midst of all kinds of adverse
circumstances. But right in
the middle of Job's painful
condition, God's promised and desired
outcome is proclaimed: "God will bring to
pass *all* that He has appointed for my life!"
And if we keep on reading to the end of the
book, we see that this proclamation of faith is

fulfilled. Job receives back twice as much as he started out with in the first place! (Job 42:10.)

Overcome Every Challenge by Faith

Notice that this verse says *God* is the One who performs that which is appointed for you. You don't have to perform it. You don't have to try to do something to make it come to pass. *He* does it!

> GOD IS THE ONE WHO PERFORMS THAT WHICH IS APPOINTED FOR YOU.

If you can lay hold of that, it will cause you to move up into a whole new realm of faith, which is exactly what God desires for you. You see, you can labor in your own strength and pray and pray and *pray,* but the thing that pleases God more than anything else is faith.

Only by faith will you come out victorious on the other side of every difficult situation you face. And rest assured, you *will* face difficult situations.

> ONLY BY FAITH WILL YOU COME OUT VICTORIOUS ON THE OTHER SIDE OF EVERY DIFFICULT SITUATION YOU FACE.

The Bible says Satan is the god of this world we live in. (2 Cor. 4:4.) That means we're all going to experience difficulties or challenges. Jesus said so Himself: **In the world ye shall have tribulation** (John 16:33). However, Jesus went on to say this: **But be of good cheer; I have overcome the world.**

So even though we're not exempt from challenges, we can still go over the top in every situation once we know who we are, what we have and what we can do in Christ. And we shouldn't just expect to win the victory every now and then. God has made it possible for us to see the end, or fulfillment, of our faith come to pass every single time!

> WE CAN GO OVER THE TOP IN EVERY SITUATION ONCE WE KNOW WHO WE ARE IN CHRIST.

We having the same spirit of faith,

according as it is written, I believed,

and therefore have I spoken;

we also believe, and therefore speak.

2 CORINTHIANS 4:13

3

DECLARING THE END BEFORE YOU BEGIN

3

DECLARING THE END
BEFORE YOU BEGIN

One thing that makes Job 23:14 such a
good Scripture to get fervent about is that Job
makes his proclamation right in the middle of
adversity. That's what the spirit of faith does.

You see, if you're going to pray effectively,
faith can't just be a message that your pastor
preaches to you every now and then. You have
to possess a *spirit* of faith.

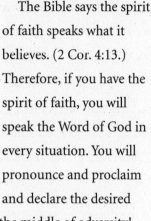

IF YOU'RE GOING TO PRAY EFFECTIVELY, YOU HAVE TO POSSESS A *SPIRIT* OF FAITH.

The Bible says the spirit of faith speaks what it believes. (2 Cor. 4:13.) Therefore, if you have the spirit of faith, you will speak the Word of God in every situation. You will pronounce and proclaim and declare the desired outcome right in the middle of adversity!

You will stand upright in the face of every form of opposition you encounter and declare the outcome. You will announce by faith how the situation you face is going to turn out. *That's* the spirit of faith!

In other words, the spirit of faith proclaims: "I see the situation. I understand that I could look at the difficulties, but it isn't over yet. And before it's over, I want to announce exactly how it's going to turn out.

"It's going to turn out with my being the head and not the tail. It's going to turn out with my being above and not beneath. It's going to turn out with my being blessed every which way—coming in and going out, up and down, in and out. That's how it's going to turn out! (Deut. 28:6,13.)

"How do I know that? Because of what Jesus did for me. Because that is my inheritance. Because victory is engraved in my heart; it is a part of my genetic makeup."

> VICTORY IS ENGRAVED IN YOUR HEART; IT IS A PART OF YOUR GENETIC MAKEUP.
>
>

Those are the words of a champion, which is exactly what the Lord has made you. Yes, you will have challenges at times, but that doesn't make you a challenger. Champions enter the ring with a different attitude than challengers. Champions already have what the challengers are trying to get—the victory!

YOUR INHERITANCE IN GOD'S KINGDOM IS ABOVE AND BEYOND ANYTHING YOU CAN DREAM, THINK OR IMAGINE.

What makes you a champion? Once you are born into the kingdom of God, you are God's workmanship, created in Christ Jesus. (Eph. 2:10.) Your inheritance in God's kingdom is above and beyond anything you can dream, think or imagine.

You are an actual partaker of His divine nature. This is the perspective from which you proclaim the end of your faith before you even begin to pray.

God Doesn't Make "Dingers"!

I heard someone say one time that Jesus is the Master and we are the "piece"—and that makes us a masterpiece! Now, it's true that we don't always feel like a masterpiece. Sometimes we feel like we're the first-grade scribbling of the Sunday school class!

But God can make a masterpiece out of first-grade scribblings. He can even take the marks the devil has put on our lives—marks we thought could never be erased—and make a beautiful painting out of them.

I once heard about a particular pastor who decided to have a flamboyant evangelist speak at his church. It was a Pentecostal church, and as you know, anything can happen in a Pentecostal church!

But there were some elderly ladies in the Pentecostal church who didn't want this evangelist to come. They told the pastor, "We don't think he ought to come here because he's too flashy."

The pastor thought about the matter and then decided, "I like this evangelist, so I'm going to have him."

So the evangelist came to the church and sat down on the front row with the pastor. At the appropriate moment, the pastor went up on the

platform and introduced the visiting minister.
As the evangelist started to walk toward the
platform, one of those little ladies stood up and
took her opportunity to "prophesy" to him.

She said, "Thus saith the Lord, 'Thou
thinkest thou art a humdinger. But thou art
not a humdinger. Thou art only a dinger!'"

That story is humorous,
but the truth is, there are
times in your life when you
feel just like a "dinger."
Nevertheless, I'm here to
tell you that if you are a
born-again Christian and
filled with the Holy Ghost,
you are a joint heir with
Jesus and you are one with

IF YOU ARE A BORN-
AGAIN CHRISTIAN,
YOU ARE A JOINT
HEIR WITH JESUS
AND ARE ONE WITH
THE WORD.

the Word. God doesn't make any "dingers." He only makes Holy Ghost humdingers!

Now, the qualities of a champion may not have totally manifested in your life yet, but they will if you'll do this: Before the desired outcome shows up, start speaking and declaring the end. Get it on the inside of you until you think it, you see it, you smell it and you speak it. Focus on God's promise until it's planted deep within you. Then it will govern your life.

FOCUS ON GOD'S PROMISE UNTIL IT'S PLANTED DEEP WITHIN YOU. THEN IT WILL GOVERN YOUR LIFE.

That is the position from which the spirit of faith prays. Before the prayer is ever spoken, you declare the outcome, *not* the problem.

Just recently, I had an opportunity to work with a woman who was dealing with a life-or-death situation. But there was one very big problem: I couldn't convince her to speak forth the end of her faith.

You see, it isn't enough that you don't say bad things. You have to speak the Word. You have to continually declare the desired outcome—not what you feel, not what your brain says, not what the unbelieving world says and surely not what the devil says—but what God says!

> YOU HAVE TO SPEAK THE WORD TO DECLARE THE DESIRED OUTCOME.

David understood this principle even as a young teenager. Remember, when he was running toward Goliath to do battle with him, he didn't do it with his mouth closed. Every step of the way, he was proclaiming the expected outcome, saying, "I'm going to take your head off and hang it in my tent!" (1 Sam. 17.)

David won the victory that day, and so will you—if you'll just make a practice of declaring what will be the end before you ever begin to pray!

For we which have believed do enter into rest, as he said, As I have sworn in my wrath, if they shall enter into my rest: although the works were finished from the foundation of the world.

HEBREWS 4:3

4

REST AND JOY: TWO KEYS TO THE FIGHT OF FAITH

4

Rest and Joy: Two Keys to the Fight of Faith

I like what a great preacher once said about prayer. He made the statement that he didn't pray more than ten minutes at a time, but he never went ten minutes without praying. Why was that true in his life? Because of his continual lifestyle of faith.

When you've truly stepped into the place of faith, there is a peace and an ease about things. The Bible says once you believe, you enter into rest. (Heb. 4:3.)

Enter Into the Rest of Faith

WHEN YOU ARE TRULY IN FAITH, ALL YOU DO IS REST AS GOD BRINGS THE ANSWER TO PASS.

When you are truly in faith, you don't have to struggle. You don't have to manipulate. You don't have to maneuver. All you have to do is just rest as God brings the answer to pass.

And you don't have to worry that your problem is too big for God to solve or that your needs are too many for Him to meet. There are absolutely no limits in God. He hasn't put you in a narrow place where needs go unmet. He has put you in a broad place of abundance, a place where anything is possible in Him!

As you learn how to stop trying to make things happen yourself and enter into the rest of faith, God will enlarge the borders of your tent. You won't stay in a transition place. You won't stay in a hard and narrow place. You'll abide in a big, broad, free place in God because in the spirit of faith, you have entered into rest.

> THE BIGGEST FIGHT OF FAITH IS LEARNING TO STOP THE STRUGGLE.
>
>

You see, the biggest fight of faith is learning to stop the fleshly struggle. The greatest challenge is to stop trying to work things out with your mind or your carnal reasoning. To enter the rest of faith, you have to stop trying to figure everything out with your education and your intelligence. And you have to stop trying to get your friends or relatives to figure it all out for you.

> MANY CHRISTIANS DON'T GRASP THE IMPORTANCE OF ENTERING INTO REST WHEN IT COMES TO WALKING BY FAITH.

You just have to decide, "God has my answer, so I'm going to rest and enjoy myself because it's a *good* fight of faith, not a *hard* fight of faith."

Many Christians just don't grasp the importance of entering into rest when it comes to walking by faith. They say, "I'm believing

God for this to come to pass; I'm fighting the good fight of faith." But that isn't what they're doing at all.

Now, these people may be fighting some kind of fight, but they're not fighting the fight of faith. I give them credit for trying hard, but they're trying hard in their own strength— and that isn't faith.

True Faith Is Filled With Joy

You see, some people pray way too fast. They may think they're in faith when they pray, but they're not. It would be so much better for them to get in faith first so they can *pray* in faith.

A prayer of faith isn't a pleading, groaning, "down under" type of prayer. It's an "up over," victorious, dominion-minded, mastery-minded prayer because, according to 1 Peter 1:7-8, true faith is filled with joy.

> **That the trial of your faith, being much more precious than of gold that perisheth, though it be tried with fire, might be found unto praise and honour and glory at the appearing of Jesus Christ: whom having not seen, ye love; in whom, though now ye see him not, yet believing, ye rejoice with joy unspeakable and full of glory.**

We're talking about what it takes to go from *believing* to *receiving* the end of your faith. So what do these verses tell you to do if you're *believing?* You are to rejoice with joy unspeakable and full of glory, *receiving.*

Some folks look so sad as they tell you, "I'm believing God to meet my need." But if they were truly believing, the Bible says they would be rejoicing with joy unspeakable and full of glory, receiving the end of their faith!

When you reach that place in God, so much joy bubbles up from the inside that you can't talk anymore. You can't sit in your seat all dignified and stuffy, thinking about your problem and worrying about how it's all going to turn out.

> WHEN YOU REACH TRUE FAITH IN GOD, SO MUCH JOY BUBBLES UP FROM THE INSIDE THAT YOU CAN'T TALK ANYMORE.

One time I was in a service when the word of the Lord came unto me, proclaiming an outcome that was the desire of my heart. I'm telling you, that word started getting bigger and bigger and bigger on the inside of me until I couldn't stand it anymore; I had to do something!

A man was sitting next to me, and I said to him, "Excuse me, sir, I have to get in the aisle. Could you just excuse me, please? I'm going to have to get in the aisle and run. I'm going to have to get in the aisle and shout. Excuse me, I'm just going to have to do something for Jesus right now."

I was so full of joy at that moment that I just had to get up and run, dance or have a little laugh in the Holy Ghost. That's called joy unspeakable and full of glory! That is when we go beyond believing and receive the end of our faith.

Some people say, "I wish God would make me dance."

But God isn't going to make you do that. He didn't make you get saved. He didn't make you tithe. He didn't make you pray in tongues. And He isn't going to make you dance. If you're going to dance, it's going to be your choice. You'll have to *choose* to dance.

I know a preacher who learned that lesson during a particular church service where everyone in his congregation suddenly cut loose and yielded to a move of the Holy Ghost. People were running, shouting and dancing in the Spirit all over the sanctuary while this preacher just stood there and watched.

The preacher prayed, *God, I wish You'd give me a dance.*

Immediately the Lord spoke to his spirit and said, "A dance is not something I give you. A dance is something *you* give *Me*."

FAITH IS WHAT
PLEASES GOD
THE MOST.

✐

Remember, faith is what pleases God the most. So when the revelation hits your heart that you have received the outcome of your faith, find some way to express your joy, and make the Father glad!

Get the Victory Before *You Pray*

The key we're talking about here is to get in faith *before* you pray. You see, when you have a spirit of faith, people can't tell what you're

going through. On the
other hand, when you don't
have a spirit of faith,
everyone can tell exactly
what you're going through
because your problems are
written all over you!

> THE KEY IS TO
> GET IN FAITH
> *BEFORE* YOU PRAY.

If you have a spirit of
faith, you rejoice regardless of circumstances.
How do you rejoice? With joy unspeakable
and full of glory. That means you're so happy,
you can hardly stand it!

One of my very favorite pray-ers in the
whole world was a woman named Mama
Lena Blackwood Cain. She went home to be
with the Lord when she was 96 years old and
still cutting her own wood for her fireplace!

I once asked her, "Mama, what is the difference between pray-ers in this generation and pray-ers in your generation?"

She replied, "The difference is that when we went to pray back then, we had the victory before we ever prayed, so we never prayed long."

Why didn't those old-time prayer warriors have to pray long? Because they already had the victory. They were already over into joy and rejoicing. God had already done what they had asked Him for, so they came to the prayer room laughing, shouting or running with joy. They had received the end of their faith, and they were happy about it!

That's what you should be experiencing as you fight *your* good fight of faith. When you're truly in faith, you see and receive the end before you even pray. That's why you can enter into the rest of God with joy unspeakable and full of glory, knowing that *God* will perform the answer that has been appointed for you!

> WHEN YOU'RE TRULY IN FAITH, YOU SEE AND RECEIVE THE END BEFORE YOU EVEN PRAY.

For we walk by faith, not by sight.

2 Corinthians 5:7

5

GIVE FAITH A PUSH

5

GIVE FAITH A PUSH

The only way we will ever see God's promises come to pass in our lives is to walk by faith every step of the way. If we want to see results, we can't afford to get tired and quit before we reach the finish line.

But sometimes we do get tired. Sometimes we need to give our faith an extra push so we can keep going. How do we do that? Well, one way we can give our faith a lift is to focus our attention on the grace of God.

You see, grace is God's grip on us, and faith is our grip on God. So as we focus on the grip He has on us, our grip on Him gets stronger.

> GRACE IS GOD'S GRIP ON US, AND FAITH IS OUR GRIP ON GOD.

"Spinning Your Wheels" Only Digs You Deeper

When I think about our faith needing an extra push, it always reminds me of an experience I had in high school back before I was saved.

My friends and I liked to go to the drive-in movies back then. There were about fifteen of us, and we didn't want to pay for several cars. So we would stop the car before we arrived at the drive-in movie. Two people would get in the front seat, two in the back seat and the rest of us would pile into the trunk. Then we would drive into the drive-in and find a place to park.

Those of us in the trunk of the car would stay in there until no one was looking and all the security personnel had gone. Then whoever was driving the car would knock on the trunk lid and tell us we could come out.

On one particular night, we all went to see *Gone With the Wind* together, and I was the driver. The drive-in that night was full to the brim, so I had to park back in the grassy area.

But it had rained the night before, and because the back of the car was so heavy, we got stuck in the mud. I opened the trunk, and everyone piled out. We all just stood there, looking at the muddy, half-buried back tires.

Someone said, "Well, the way to get them out is just to rev up the car."

But do you know what happens if you get stuck in the mud and you keep spinning your wheels in the same place? You just dig yourself in deeper and deeper. And if you don't give that car a big shove to push it out, the whole back end will eventually sink down in the mud.

Unfortunately, it took me and my friends a long time to figure that out. We made the situation a lot worse by spinning our wheels before we ever made it better!

In the same way, we often spin our spiritual "wheels" in the midst of our adversity, letting our problems consume our thoughts and our words. But that only makes the situation worse. We'll never get to the end of our faith by spinning around in the problem, sinking deeper and deeper into defeat. When we find ourselves making that mistake, we have to do something to jumpstart our faith so we can get out of the "mud" of our circumstances.

> WE OFTEN SPIN OUR SPIRITUAL "WHEELS" IN THE MIDST OF OUR ADVERSITY, LETTING OUR PROBLEMS CONSUME OUR THOUGHTS AND OUR WORDS.

How do we do that? No matter what kind of adversity we might be going through, we get out by speaking God's Word on the

> NO MATTER WHAT KIND OF ADVERSITY WE MIGHT BE GOING THROUGH, WE GET OUT BY SPEAKING GOD'S WORD ON THE MATTER.

matter. Our words will give our faith a shove and push us right out of that muddy mess into joy unspeakable and full of glory. That joy will give us the strength we need to finish the race and see the end of our faith.

The Joy of the Lord Is Our Strength

I remember one particular night when the Lord spoke to my heart about the power of joy. Something was on my mind bothering me, and as I lay there on my bed, trying to get to sleep, the Lord said, "I told you that the joy of the Lord is your strength. How else am I going to give you strength in your inner man except with joy?"

Have you ever thought about that? How else is God going to strengthen you except with joy? Since the joy of the Lord is your strength, you need to get some joy if you want to reach the end of your faith!

If you don't start rejoicing, you could get stuck somewhere in the middle of your fight of faith. You might still receive some blessings. But I'm telling you, you'll get so much more if you finish!

So make the decision that you're not going to stop until you've reached the end of your faith. Instead of getting stuck in the mud of your circumstances, give your faith a push by

MAKE THE DECISION THAT YOU'RE NOT GOING TO STOP UNTIL YOU'VE REACHED THE END OF YOUR FAITH.

speaking God's Word. And whenever you start feeling weak or discouraged, remember the solution God has provided for you. Let the joy of the Lord rise up inside of you and give you supernatural strength!

Now unto him that is able to do
exceeding abundantly above
all that we ask or think, according
to the power that worketh in us.

EPHESIANS 3:20

6

RECEIVE THE FULLNESS OF WHAT GOD HAS FOR YOU

6

RECEIVE THE FULLNESS OF WHAT GOD HAS FOR YOU

One more thing you must understand in order to push through every barrier and receive the fullness of what you're believing God for is this:

God is not a generalities type of God. He is a God of great detail.

He doesn't care much for vague, general prayers. He likes it when we believe Him for

GOD DOESN'T CARE
MUCH FOR VAGUE,
GENERAL PRAYERS.

✑❧

precise, detailed results. That way when He shows forth His faithfulness and manifests the answer, we can know without a doubt that we have received the exact outcome we desire.

Receiving Exactly What I Desired

Let me share an illustration from my own life that's a good example of this truth. Before our church built a new office building to house all our ministry offices, the ministry staff occupied a total of five buildings.

In those five office buildings, everyone had an office that fit his or her personality. Some people had stars on their ceilings. Other people had stripes on the walls. Some people had football players on the wall. Some had black-lacquered, contemporary furniture. Others had "early attic" décor.

Some people had "Precious Moments" decorating their offices. Other people had flowers sticking out of frames. It looked like some had rats in their couches. Others had no couches at all.

In the middle of the building program, I heard through the ministry "grapevine" that we would be moving all that old furniture and décor into our new offices.

That news didn't make me very happy. You see, when we began this project, I'd had a little talk with Jesus, but I didn't tell Him about my troubles! I told Him how it was going to be in this building according to His Word. After all, He is the One who gave us the vision in the first place!

Of course, I realize that, as pastor, my husband, Mac, has to look at the church finances all the time to decide how best to spend the money that comes in. But I also know that as a local body, we are coming into the land of more than enough—a place in God where we don't have to look at the financial ledger every day and decide what goes where.

We are moving toward the end of our faith. We are learning to receive and live according to the high standard that would please our God.

So whenever I heard someone say, "We're moving that old furniture into the new building," I'd go to the Father with joy unspeakable and pray, "Lord, I want to thank You for all my new furniture to match my new building. I thank You, Lord, that we're not moving that old furniture into this new building." On a regular basis I'd pray, "Lord, You see our nice, new building. Thank You for my new furniture."

One day as the time approached for our move into the new office building, Mac came in to talk to me. I could tell by his eyes that he was about to break the bad news to me as easily as he could.

"You know, Honey," he began, "we've spent so much money on that building...."

I whirled around and said, "Mac Hammond, you know what we're believing for. We are believing for new furniture."

Mac backtracked fast: "Yes, you're right. Okay, that's what we'll keep standing in faith for."

It wasn't long after that conversation that God showed us the way to the end of our faith regarding this matter of brand-new office furniture.

Throughout the time our office building was being constructed, our church prayer group had been praying. During these prayer sessions, two words had been coming up in our prayers for quite a while: "metro systems." (In our church, we pray a little differently than others might. We pray by the Holy Ghost, and then later we often find out what we were praying about.)

Soon after Mac's talk with me about the new office furniture, someone came to me

and said something about a business called
Metro Systems. He explained that it is a
company that leases furniture and sets up an
entire office complex exactly the way their
clients want it.

I was skeptical at first, but I said, "All right,
let's go on down to Metro Systems and see
what it is."

When I first arrived at Metro Systems, I
was amazed. God was written all over their
furniture! We were able to pick out the exact
furniture we wanted—color, style and
everything. We leased the furniture, and they
came in and set everything up.

And do you know what else? We were able to
do it! We could handle the cost of leasing all

> MOVE YOUR
> FAITH UP A FEW
> NOTCHES AND START
> BELIEVING GOD FOR
> OUR SPECIFIC,
> DETAILED NEEDS TO
> BE MET.

that beautiful furniture. The whole thing was an absolute miracle of God in every detail. Otherwise, we might still be looking at the middle of adversity instead of the end of our faith! So let's move our faith up a few notches and start believing God for our specific, detailed needs to be met.

Move On Up to Who You Are in Christ!

Someone might say, "Well, Sister Lynne, it's hard for me to do that. You see, I have a history of failure and disappointment. So it's difficult for me to get my hopes up."

If that's the case, get rid of that history. Put it under the blood of Jesus, and then get it out of your mind and out of your mouth. Instead of talking about your past, continually speak forth what *God* says about who you are, what you have and what you can do in Christ.

> INSTEAD OF TALKING ABOUT YOUR PAST, CONTINUALLY SPEAK FORTH WHAT *GOD* SAYS ABOUT WHO YOU ARE.

I once talked to a thirty-year-old woman who was still struggling inside because of something that had happened to her in the fourth grade. On that day many years before, a classmate had called her a "fatso." She told me that those words in the fourth grade had made a stain on her soul that she couldn't seem to get over. She had even been going to a psychiatrist for a number of years, trying to find some help for her problem.

I asked her, "Are you born again?"

"Yes," she replied.

I said, "Well, then, that stain is gone. You're a new creation in Christ Jesus. Old things have passed away. There is nothing from the past that can hold you in bondage if Jesus has set you free."

That's true for you as well, my friend. You know, Jesus went to a lot of trouble to do what He did for you on the Cross. You've been born again into the kingdom of God. You're a new creature with new ways and new approaches. You have a new life, a new spirit, a new love, a new glory. You don't ever have to be controlled by what the world or the devil says!

You are not the product of what someone else says. You are not the product of some genetic determiner. You are a new creation in Christ. Old things have passed away, and all things have become new.

Your identification is not even with your natural parents. Your identification is in Jesus, the Anointed One, the King of Kings and the Lord of Lords.

You're a child of the King, a joint heir with Jesus, and you are one with the Word. You are a righteous

> YOUR IDENTIFICATION IS IN JESUS, THE ANOINTED ONE, THE KING OF KINGS AND THE LORD OF LORDS.

one. You are transformed and transfigured, and you have a bright future. You are forgiven, and your sins are forgotten. There are no limits to how far you can go in God, for Jesus has set you free!

So make sure that the words you think and speak about yourself agree with what God says about you. Let those words build a strong spirit of faith in your heart. Then get ready to move up to a higher place in God, where you can receive the end of your faith!

Hold On to the End

I want to emphasize one last point about receiving the outcome of your faith: *You have to hold on to the end.* There is a beginning to your faith, and there is also an end. Very few people ever reach the end of their faith. It's great to start walking by faith, but the greatest thing is to *finish*.

So let me give you a few more Scriptures to help you hold on to the end in your own fight of faith. I want to give you enough ammunition so you can blow the devil clean out of the water when he tries to discourage you and make you give up!

First, Luke 1:45 is a wonderful Scripture to get fervent about:

> **And blessed is she that believed: for there shall be a performance of those things which were told her from the Lord.**

YOU HAVE TO HOLD ON TO THE END.

Then in Romans 4:20, we see how Abraham was able to receive the end of *his* faith:

He staggered not at the promise of God through unbelief; but was strong in faith, giving glory to God.

Abraham was fully persuaded; therefore, he just kept praising God and rejoicing. He knew that since God promised it, He would perform it!

I like Ephesians 3:20 too. It says that God **... is able to do exceeding abundantly above all that we ask or think, according to the power that worketh in us.**

Why does that divine power work in you? Why do the angels of God work for you? Because of your steadfast believing. As you hold on to the end, the angels go to work to bring an answer that is far beyond what you could dare ask or imagine.

Second Timothy 1:12 says this:

> For I know whom I have believed, and am persuaded that he is able to keep that which I have committed unto him against that day.

God is able to keep the end of your faith safe from every adversity until that day when you see Jesus face to face. Why? Because **faithful is he that calleth you, who also will do it** (1 Thess. 5:24).

BECAUSE OF YOUR STEADFAST BELIEVING, THE ANGELS GO TO WORK TO BRING AN ANSWER THAT IS FAR BEYOND WHAT YOU COULD DARE ASK OR IMAGINE.

Finally, Jude 24,25 tells you how to put yourself in a position for God to bring to pass all He has planned for your life:

> Now unto him that is able to keep you from falling, and to present you faultless before the presence of his glory with exceeding joy...be glory and majesty, dominion and power.

IT IS IN THE PRESENCE OF GOD'S GLORY THAT YOUR FAITH COMES ALIVE AND YOU FIND FULLNESS OF JOY.

It is in the presence of God's glory that your faith comes alive and you find fullness of joy. That's the place where you should live each moment of every day. That's the place where God is able to perform that which is appointed for you.

But never forget—He's the One who does it! Your part is to declare the outcome before you ever begin; to rejoice that the answer is yours to claim; to hold on to the end, no matter what adversity comes your way.

As you do your part, God will do His. Surely He will bring to pass the end of your faith!

ABOUT THE AUTHOR

Lynne Hammond is nationally known for her teaching and writing on the subject of prayer. The desire of Lynne's heart is to impart the spirit of prayer to churches and nations throughout the world. Her books include *Secrets to Powerful Prayer, When Healing Doesn't Come Easily, Dare To Be Free* and *The Master Is Calling*.

She is the host and teacher for *A Call to Prayer*, a weekly European television broadcast, and is an occasional guest teacher on her husband's national weekly television broadcast, *The Winner's Way With Mac Hammond*. She also regularly writes articles on the subject of prayer in *Winner's Way* magazine and publishes a newsletter called *Prayer Notes* for people of prayer. Lynne is a frequent speaker at national prayer conferences and meetings around the country.

Lynne and her husband, Mac, are founders of Living Word Christian Center, a large and growing church in Minneapolis, Minnesota. Under Lynne's leadership at Living Word, the prayer ministry has become a nationally recognized model for developing effective "pray-ers."

To contact Lynne Hammond,
write:

Lynne Hammond

Mac Hammond Ministries

P.O. Box 29469

Minneapolis, Minnesota 55429

Please include your prayer requests
and comments when you write.

OTHER BOOKS BY
LYNNE HAMMOND

Spiritual Enrichment Series:
When God Invades the Earth
A Place Called "In the Spirit"
The Hour of No Impossibility

Secrets to Powerful Prayer:
Discovering the Languages of the Heart

When Healing Doesn't Come Easily

The Master Is Calling:
Discovering the Wonders of Spirit-Led Prayer

Dare To Be Free

Available from your local bookstore.

HARRISON HOUSE
Tulsa, Oklahoma 74153

Prayer of Salvation

A born-again, committed relationship with God is the key to the victorious life. Jesus, the Son of God, laid down His life and rose again so that we could spend eternity with Him in heaven and experience His absolute best on earth. The Bible says, **For God so loved the world, that he gave his only begotten Son, that whosoever believeth in him should not perish, but have everlasting life** (John 3:16).

It is the will of God that everyone receive eternal salvation. The way to receive this salvation is to call upon the name of Jesus and confess Him as your Lord. The Bible says, **That if thou shalt confess with thy mouth the Lord Jesus, and shalt believe in thine heart that God hath raised him from the dead, thou shalt be saved. For whosoever shall call upon the name of the Lord shall be saved** (Romans 10:9-10,13).

Jesus has given salvation, healing and countless benefits to all who call upon His name. These benefits can be yours if you receive Him into your heart by praying this prayer:

Heavenly Father, I come to You admitting that I am a sinner. Right now, I choose to turn away from sin, and I ask You to cleanse me of all unrighteousness. I believe that Your Son, Jesus, died on the cross to take away my sins. I also believe that He rose again from the dead so that I may be justified and made righteous through faith in Him. I call upon the name of Jesus Christ to be the Savior and Lord of my life. Jesus, I choose to follow You, and I ask that You fill me with the power of the Holy Spirit. I declare that right now, I am a born-again child of God. I am free from sin and full of the righteousness of God. I am saved in Jesus' name, Amen.

If you have prayed this prayer to receive Jesus Christ as your Savior, or if this book has changed your life, we would like to hear from you. Please write us at:

Harrison House Publishers
P.O. Box 35035
Tulsa, Oklahoma 74153

You can also visit us on the web at
www.harrisonhouse.com

THE HARRISON HOUSE VISION

Proclaiming the truth and the power

Of the Gospel of Jesus Christ

With excellence;

Challenging Christians to

Live victoriously,

Grow spiritually,

Know God intimately.